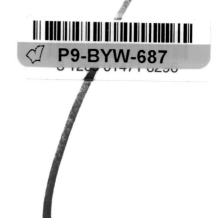

Jun 2015

A FIRST LOOK AT AMERICA'S PRESIDENTS

JAMES MADISON

The 4th President

by Josh Gregory

Consultant: Meena Bose
Director, Peter S. Kalikow Center for the Study of the American Presidency
Peter S. Kalikow Chair in Presidential Studies
Professor, Political Science
Hofstra University
Hempstead, New York

BEARPORT
PUBLISHING

New York, New York

Credits

Cover, © GL Archive/Alamy; 4, Courtesy of the Library of Congress; 5, Courtesy of the White House Historical Association/Wikimedia Commons; 6, The Design Lab; 7, Courtesy of the Library of Congress; 8, © North Wind Picture Archives/Alamy; 9T, Courtesy of the Library of Congress/Wikimedia Commons; 9B, U.S. National Guard/Wikimedia Commons; 10, The Indian Reporter/Wikimedia Commons; 11, © INSADCO Photography/Alamy; 12, Courtesy of the White House Historical Association/Wikimedia Commons; 13, © North Wind Picture Archives/Alamy; 14, © North Wind Picture Archives/Alamy; 15T, Courtesy of the White House Historical Association/Wikimedia Commons; 15B, © Glasshouse Images/Alamy; 16, © Stock Montage, Inc./Alamy; 17T, Courtesy of the Library of Congress; 17B, Mmxx/Wikimedia Commons; 18, George G. Milford/Wikimedia Commons; 19T, Courtesy of the Library of Congress; 19B, Courtesy of the National Numismatic Collection/National Museum of American History; 20, Courtesy of the U.S. National Guard/Wikimedia Commons; 21L, © Glasshouse Images/Alamy; 22, Courtesy of the Library of Congress; 23T, The Design Lab; 23B, Courtesy of the Library of Congress.

Publisher: Kenn Goin
Editor: Joyce Tavolocci
Creative Director: Spencer Brinker
Design: The Design Lab
Photo Researcher: Josh Gregory

Special thanks to fifth-grader Lucy Barr and second-grader Brian Barr for their help in reviewing this book.

Library of Congress Cataloging-in-Publication Data

Gregory, Josh.
  James Madison: the 4th President / by Josh Gregory ; consultant, Meena Bose, Director, Peter S. Kalikow Center for the Study of the American Presidency, Peter S. Kalikow Chair in Presidential Studies, Professor, political science, Hofstra University, Hempstead, New York.
      pages cm. — (A first look at America's Presidents)
  Includes index.
  ISBN 978-1-62724-559-3 (library binding) — ISBN 1-62724-559-6 (library binding)
  1. Madison, James, 1751–1836—Juvenile literature. 2. Presidents—United States—Biography—Juvenile literature. I. Bose, Meenekshi, 1970– II. Title. III. Title: James Madison, the fourth President.
  E342.G76 2015
  973.5'1092—dc23 [B]   2014034553

For more information, write to Bearport Publishing Company, Inc., 45 West 21st Street, Suite 3B, New York, New York 10010. Printed in the United States of America.

10 9 8 7 6 5 4 3 2 1

CONTENTS

President and Leader

James Madison was president when the United States was still young. Madison helped create the country's government and laws. He also led the fight against Great Britain during the War of 1812.

The War of 1812 lasted from 1812 to 1815.

James Madison was the fourth president. He served from 1809 to 1817.

A Love of Learning

James Madison was born in 1751 in the **colony** of Virginia. He was the oldest of 12 children. James loved to learn. He studied math, science, and languages. He also learned about the law.

In the 1700s, there were 13 American colonies. The colonies were ruled by Britain.

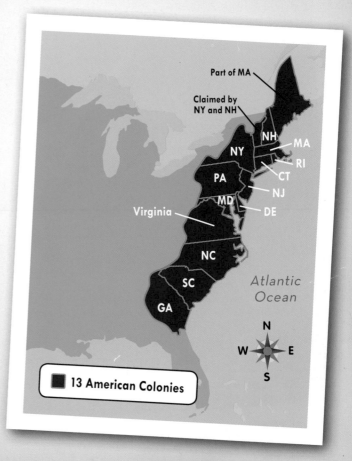

13 American Colonies

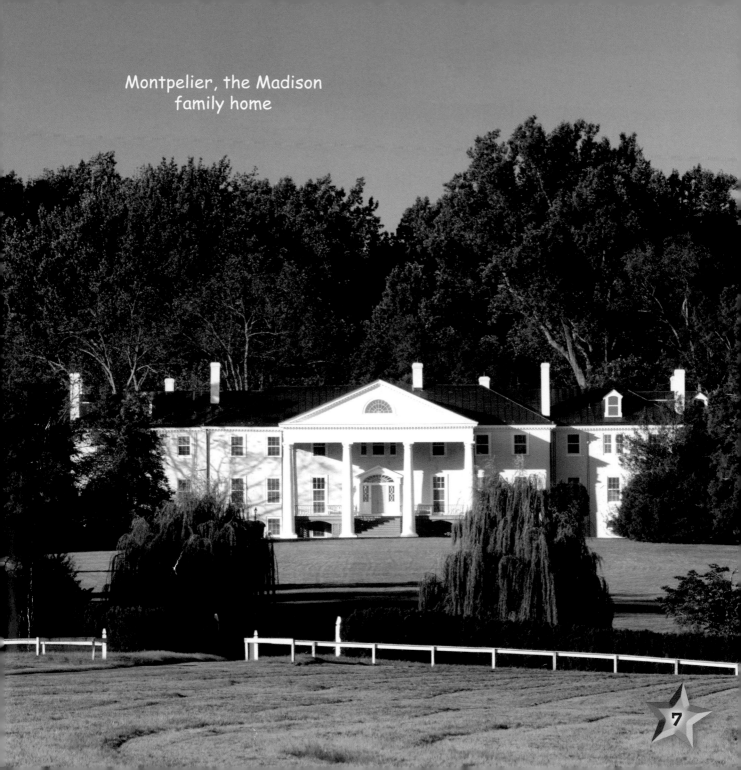

Montpelier, the Madison family home

A War for Freedom

In the 1770s, the colonies were unhappy with British rule. They fought a war for freedom from Britain. That led to the birth of the United States. Madison had many ideas about how to form a new government. He wrote about them. People began to think of him as a leader.

Americans thought that British laws and taxes were unfair.

Madison became well known during the war for America's freedom.

The war was called the Revolutionary War. It lasted from 1775 to 1783.

American soldiers fire on British troops.

Creating the Constitution

After the war, Americans had to decide how to run their new country. Madison met with other leaders in Philadelphia. They wrote a **text** called the **Constitution**. It was a plan for the government and its laws.

Madison and other leaders met in 1787 to write the Constitution.

Madison also helped write ten amendments. These were added to the Constitution. They are called the Bill of Rights. They protect important freedoms.

Congress OF THE United States

begun and held at the City of New York, on

Wednesday the Fourth of March, one thousand seven hundred and eighty nine

The Bill of Rights was added to the Constitution in 1791.

Becoming President

Madison's actions and ideas had made him famous. In 1808, he ran for president. Madison easily won. In 1809, he moved to the **White House** in Washington, D.C.

Washington, D.C., became the U.S. capital in 1800. Before that, first New York City and then Philadelphia had served as the capital.

James Madison's wife, Dolley, was a popular first lady.

Madison was sworn in as president in 1809.

Another War

As president, Madison faced another war. In 1812, the United States fought Britain again. British troops entered the capital in 1814. They burned down many buildings. The White House was one of them.

British troops in Washington, D.C., during the War of 1812

Madison led the country during the War of 1812.

Dolley was at the White House when the British attacked. She escaped to safety.

Fire and smoke badly damaged the White House.

Rebuilding the Capital

U.S. soldiers bravely fought the British. The United States won the war in 1815. Americans were proud of their president. They felt the country was stronger than ever.

The Battle of New Orleans was the final battle of the War of 1812.

It took three years to rebuild the White House.

After serving as president, Madison returned to his family's farm in Virginia. He died there in 1836.

Remembering Madison

Today, we remember Madison as a great American. He led the country through war. He also helped shape the government and laws of the United States. His ideas still guide our country.

Statues of James and Dolley Madison at Montpelier

Today, people can see a copy of the Constitution from 1787. It is in Washington, D.C.

Madison's face appears on the $5,000 bill. The bill is no longer printed today.

TIMELINE

Here are some major events from James Madison's life.

1787
Madison helps write the Constitution.

1775–1783
The American colonies battle Great Britain in the Revolutionary War.

1751
Madison is born in the colony of Virginia.

1750   1760   1770   1780   1790

1791
Congress adds Madison's Bill of Rights to the Constitution.

1809
Madison begins his
first term as president.

1812–1815
Madison leads the United
States against Britain
in the War of 1812.

| 1800 | 1810 | 1820 | 1830 | 1840 |

1817
Madison's time as
president ends.

1836
Madison dies at
home in Virginia.

FACTS and QUOTES

After his presidency, Madison helped run the University of Virginia.

"If men were angels, no government would be necessary."

"Knowledge will forever govern ignorance."

Madison was a small man. He was only about five feet four inches (1.6 m) tall and weighed around 100 pounds (45 kg).

JAMES MADISON
1751–1836

GLOSSARY

13 American Colonies

amendments (uh-MEND-muhnts) changes that are made to a law

capital (KAP-uh-tuhl) a city where a country's government is based

colony (KOL-uh-nee) an area that has been settled by people from another country and is ruled by that country

Constitution (*kon*-stuh-TOO-shuhn) the document containing the basic laws of the United States

text (TEKST) a written work

White House (WITE HOUSS) the official home of the president of the United States

Index

Read More

Pearl, Norman. *The Bill of Rights (American Symbols).* Minneapolis, MN: Picture Window Books (2007).

Venezia, Mike. *James Madison (Getting to Know the U.S. Presidents).* New York: Children's Press (2004).

Learn More Online

To learn more about James Madison, visit
www.bearportpublishing.com/AmericasPresidents

About the Author:
Josh Gregory writes and edits books for kids. He lives in Chicago, Illinois.